# HAUNTED CAPE MAY

## Lynda Lee Macken

# HAUNTED CAPE MAY

ISBN 0-9700718-5-X

All photos taken by the author.

Book cover design by Jo Butz, *Graphic Design Studio*.

Back cover graphic by *CatStuff*.

Printed on recycled paper by Sheridan Books.

## CONTENTS

## FOREWORD

The "nation's oldest seaside resort" is known for its gently sloping beaches, cooling ocean breezes, remarkable Victorian architecture and GHOSTS!

While researching stories for *Ghosts of the Garden State* it soon became apparent that Cape May harbored *more* than her share of specters. So, just *why is Cape May so haunted?*

Since 1766 Cape May's oceanfront has been famous for invigorating the spirits of sea bathers. Because of her long history of spectral visitations, it's plausible that the mist-laden atmosphere is responsible for enlivening the spirits of the long dead as well.

Cape May has had its share of tragedy. Pirates and wreckers ravaged the seaside enclave, the Civil War took its toll, and fires and floods plagued the peninsula. More reasons the area is embedded with the residual energy of so many spirits.

The Victorians followed elaborate mourning practices and observed a lengthy bereavement. Even men wore large beautiful lockets bearing tiny mourning pictures of figures weeping over tombs.

This was a society who was reluctant to let go and this might be why so many spirits hang on.

Another important aspect of the Victorian Age, and perhaps a stimulus for the phantom populace, was the popular belief in Spiritualism – the ability to communicate with the dead. Inspired by Queen Victoria and Mary Todd Lincoln, séances, automatic writing, and Ouija boards were some of the methods used to contact the dearly departed.

Hauntings are the other side of Spiritualism – the tables are turned and the dead endeavor to communicate with the living!

The Victorians longed for proof of life after death and they took their quest quite seriously. Have the seekers found their long sought answer and stay on to share the existence of an afterlife with the living?

The city by the sea has been home to millions of summer residents since the mid 18th century. Since most of the paranormal activity occurred during and after the refurbishing of the old houses, it could be that the physical changes in the structures "woke up" the sleeping specters and released their dormant energy.

Cape May's specters are not the traditional threatening type. For the most part, the spirits are

"Victorian" in nature, reserved and well mannered. They don't drag chains or let out blood curdling screams and moans. They mean no harm and make no demands. No ill tempered *"Get out of here!"* commands, only barely discernable whispers and sighs. No clamoring for attention – just a quiet co-existence where death dropped them off.

A visit to Cape May is a step back in time when life was lived at a slower pace. Visitors find it easy to relax and achieve an altered state. Many who have seen through the veil and glimpsed the ghosts in the seaside town have been caught off guard when the spirits appear. A peek into this other world, that some contend concurrently exists with ours, happens when it's least expected.

The stories in this volume are about the startling manifestations by those who have gone before. The spirits who linger seem to be living out otherworldly lives at their former haunts, albeit in another dimension. The ghosts who haunt historic Cape May continue to go about their existence oblivious to the fact that decades have passed – and so have they.

*There's more than meets the eye inside Congress Hall.*

## CONGRESS HALL
Congress Street & Beach Drive

Originally called Cape Island, the peninsula was first settled by whalers in the 1600s. Since the 18th century the area was a known resort and residents from the neighboring cities of Baltimore, Philadelphia, and Wilmington sojourned to the Cape Island community to take advantage of the cooler clime.

The locals housed them and fed them and unwittingly established a new business venture – tourism. More and more, people came to fish, pick shells, and ride their carriages on the peninsula's hard packed sand beaches.

Thomas H. Hughes was the first to build a guesthouse for the sea-bathers. In 1816, at the corner of Congress Street and Beach Drive, Hughes erected a three story "barn-like" boardinghouse. Guests ate in the first floor dining hall and bunked in the two top floors. Lodging at the time was rustic – the structures were unpainted outside and unfinished inside.

Hughes was the first Cape May County resident elected to Congress and he officially renamed his guesthouse "Congress Hall" in 1828.

The Congress Hall that stands today is the third one to bear the name and is constructed of brick, since flames devoured the first two wooden structures.

At one time Cape May was called the *"playground of presidents."* Ulysses S. Grant vacationed here in 1873 and Chester A. Arthur stayed in 1893.

Congress Hall was host to James Buchanan, Benjamin Harrison, and Franklin Pierce. Harrison had Congress Hall set up as his summer White House. With Harrison in residence, John Philip Sousa was inspired to compose *The Congress Hall March* on the premises, and premiered the piece on the lodge's sweeping front lawn.

Congress Hall has just undergone a $22 million historic rehabilitation to bring the L-shaped landmark back to her former glory. The interior of the hotel will reflect the 1920s era.

Before her recent renovation, Congress Hall stood empty. Or did it?

Not according to clairvoyant Gail Farace. Jennifer Kopp reported in the *Cape May Star and*

*Wave* on an investigation conducted by the psychic inside the building before it closed for renovation. During her visit Ferace discerned a woman from an earlier day toting a parasol. The Victorian era female beckoned Farace to follow...the spirit, visible only to the psychic, led the way to the lobby where Farace intuited that the spirit was trying to communicate a message.

At the time, the psychic was unable to discern what the wraith wanted to convey. The spectral lady eventually faded away.

The next day, a fire erupted in the lobby, but was quickly controlled and caused little damage. Only then did the psychic understand.

*The Colvmns by the Sea is home to those
who have gone before.*

## COLVMNS BY THE SEA
1513 Beach Drive

The exterior Italianate columns inspired the name of this turn-of-the-century palazzo style mansion built in 1905 by prominent Philadelphia physician, Dr. Charles Davis and his wife Emily.

The interior design offers fluted, hand-carved coffered ceilings and a grand, three-story, cherry wood staircase.

Sitting on the sweeping porch, captivated by the surging sea, one can easily conjure up the days of pirates and sailors and tall ships.

When the Rein family bought the property in the 1980s and began to renovate, unexplainable condensation appeared on an interior wall. They called in a plumber to determine the cause of the moisture, but the situation could not be explained.

Psychics offered the cosmic theory that the building was weeping as it made the transition from private home to public hostelry.

Bernadette Kaschner and her husband have owned the Colvmns by the Sea since 1994. In the early years of her proprietorship, Ms. Kaschner had some disconcerting encounters. Her experiences occurred while she was performing "boring," mindless tasks.

One day as she was clearing dishes she spotted an older gentleman sitting at a dining room table. He seemed very peaceful and stared straight ahead oblivious to Kaschner's presence. The man seemed to be waiting for something – lunch, maybe? Bernadette noted that he was wearing a 1920s style woolen suit, totally inappropriate for the hot summer day.

The proprietor hurried into the kitchen with the dirty dishes and quickly returned to address the man. When she entered the dining room, he was gone. No way could he have gotten up that quickly and exited the room. She looked everywhere but he was nowhere to be seen.

Another time as she prepared for dinner, absently dicing tomatoes in the kitchen, she heard the back door open. In walked a woman dressed in a long gray skirt, high-necked white blouse and a loose-fitting gray jacket. The woman walked through the pantry into the kitchen, passed Ms. Kaschner and continued down the hall. Bernadette stared in disbelief at the unknown woman. This was not a registered guest, so Kaschner went off to follow the stranger, but the unfamiliar woman was gone. The lady in gray disappeared in the blink of an eye.

The Davis' grandson Jim visits The Colvmns every year to once again enjoy his summer home, the site of many happy times. Davis, one of nine children, relives scenes from his childhood by sharing memories and telling stories of life as it was in Cape May seventy years ago.

Bernadette asked him about the type of dress the Davis' Irish maids wore back then. He shared that they wore long, gray skirts, high-collared blouses and long, loose gray jackets. The description confirmed Bernadette's suspicion that the woman she witnessed was a Davis servant.

Davis related that his grandmother had suffered a stroke, so she stayed in a ground floor room. He recalls how he and his eight siblings would often visit with her. This is the spot where Bernadette has discerned the sound of unseen children playing. Psychics felt an overwhelming sense of sadness in the room and perceived an older woman in bed.

The Kaschners feel protected by the spirits that subtly pervade their space and relish their role as guardians preserving a part of Cape May's past.

Henry Washington Sawyer constructed Cape May's
Chalfonte Hotel in 1875. Residents in his Cold Spring house
claimed his apparition appeared at the top of the stairs.

## HENRY WASHINGTON SAWYER HOMESTEAD

Cape May lies south of the imaginary Mason-Dixon Line, yet her loyalty was with the Union during the Civil War.

Henry Washington Sawyer came to Cape Island from Pennsylvania in 1848 lured by the blooming tourist trade. A carpenter by trade, he was also a born patriot as his name suggests. When the War Between the States broke out, he was first in line to volunteer.

Quickly advancing to the rank of second lieutenant, Sawyer re-enlisted as a captain after his three-month stint ended, and was assigned to the First New Jersey Calvary Division.

Unfortunately wounded in battle in Virginia, he was captured by the Confederates and sent to Libby Prison in Richmond where he was destined to meet a grim fate.

The confederates gathered the imprisoned officers and informed them that two would be chosen by lottery to die in retaliation for two Confederate officers lost in battle. Sawyer's name was first drawn. He staunchly accepted his doom.

With only eight days to live, he was allowed a visit from his wife and children. He wrote her of his plight and implored her to come.

Realizing the seriousness of the situation, she beseeched influential Cape Island friends to intercede on her husband's behalf. The matter went all the way to the White House where President Lincoln directed his Secretary of War to detain two confederate officers. General William Henry Fitzhugh Lee, son of General Robert E. Lee, and General Winder, son of the Confederate Provost Marshall General, were taken hostage.

The message was delivered loud and clear to the Confederacy - execute Sawyer or any other guiltless captive, and Lee and Winder would die.

Infuriated by the threat, the Confederacy nevertheless relented and eventually exchanged Sawyer for Lee's son.

Sawyer was reunited with his Calvary, achieved the rank of colonel, and at the war's end returned to his beloved Cape Island.

The "Colonel," as he was called, went on to construct the beautiful Chalfonte Hotel, which he operated for seventeen years.

Sawyer lived out his final years on his large Seashore Road plantation in Cold Spring.

By the year 2000, all that physically remained of the homestead was an abandoned house, which unfortunately was demolished that summer.

Those who had resided in the 1858 dwelling claimed to have had unforgettable encounters with the spiritual remains of Colonel Sawyer. Most times when the gentleman's ghost was witnessed his full-bodied apparition stood at the top of the staircase.

Before the place was leveled writer Jennifer Kopp, psychic medium Gail Farace, and historian Clark Donlin paid a visit to the historic home. Kopp reported on their field trip in the *Cape May Star and Wave.*

Farace was first to feel the cold spots and see the grayish mist or ectoplasm. The psychic was able to identify the cloudy forms as the spirits of Henry Sawyer's second wife, Mary Emma, and their son, Henry Washington Sawyer, 2nd.

Mary Emma's spirit was directing the visitors to the living room where her husband had been laid out in his coffin, a common practice before there were funeral "homes." Maybe Mary Emma thought the modern day guests were mourners coming to pay their respects.

*Angel of the Sea B & B - Cape May's largest and one of the most haunted.*

## ANGEL OF THE SEA
7 Trenton Avenue

William Weightman Sr. was a Philadelphia chemist who discovered and manufactured medical quinine. Around 1850 he built a magnificent "summer cottage" in the center of town. Today his mansion is known as the Angel of the Sea B & B.

This architectural treasure was originally erected on the corner of Franklin and Washington Streets. Thirty years later, Weightman's son wanted an ocean view, so he hired local farmers to relocate the house to the corner of Ocean and Beach Avenues.

Too large to move in one piece, the farmers cut the structure in half and moved it in two sections. Literally using only "horsepower," mules and horses, the men labored throughout the winter pulling the two sections of the house on rolling tree trunks. When the house reached its destination, the workers met with an impasse. They hadn't figured that although the animals were good for "pulling" the house, they were of no use in "pushing" the house back together again!

Good weather was approaching, Weightman would soon arrive, and the men needed to get back to their farms. They quickly attached the two sections together as the structure appears today.

Upon Weightman's death in 1907, the house was sold and operated as the Lafayette Hotel.

When the Great March Storm devastated Cape May in 1962, the structure was severely damaged and barely survived. The decision was made to bulldoze the two buildings and a cinderblock motel, able to withstand the elements, would be the (pitiful) replacement.

Enter Reverend Carl McIntire, the charismatic head of the International Council of Christian Churches. When McIntire laid eyes on Cape May, it was love at first sight. He felt the quintessential American seaside resort was the perfect spot to headquarter his mission of *"putting more Patriotism in the Christians and more Christianity in the Patriots."* McIntire salvaged the building.

So yet another move was on the horizon for the onerous structure. In October 1963, McIntire, in his trademark showman fashion, broadcasted his radio program from the front porch of the building as it slowly made its way down Beach Drive on flatbed trucks!

The landmark was set at an angle at the present Beach Drive and Trenton Street location.

From 1962 to 1981, the houses were used to board McIntire's workforce employed at his other holdings, the Christian Admiral Hotel and Congress Hall, along with students from the minister's Shelton College. During this time, a tragedy transpired which could explain the paranormal phenomena inside the Angel of the Sea.

The story goes that a young woman, known only as "Miss Brown," dormered at the Lafayette. One fateful night she arrived after curfew only to realize she had left her keys at the Christian Admiral where she worked. Rules were strict so she considered her options. She figured a way out - she could climb up the fire escape, then over to her window.

Miss Brown easily reached her destination but as she struggled to remove the unwieldy screen she lost her balance and fell to her death.

Some imaginative guests swear they hear the young woman knocking on the windows during the night frantic to get in, but that is contrary to Miss Brown's good-natured, post-mortem pranks.

The spirit likes to play typical teenage tricks. Televisions and lights go on and off when no one is in the room; not surprisingly, doors lock and unlock of their own accord, and objects put down in one place are found somewhere else hours later.

Employees at Cape May's largest bed and breakfast have a place in their heart for Miss Brown, their "angel" whose spirit pervades the inn.

There are those who assert that the Angel of the Sea shelters more than one ghost. Some say the atmosphere holds the spirit of a former owner's daughter and she's the one responsible for the phantom pranks. Some feel another revenant who remains behind is a soldier who was housed in the building and died of tuberculosis on the premises. Could he be the one causing the spirit shenanigans?

Regardless of who or how many wraiths reside inside the Angel of the Sea, photos taken inside the B & B reveal orbs of light thought to be the actual manifestation of ghostly energy.

## HOTEL CAPE MAY

Cape May's "gilded age" was a time of elegant hotels, lavish seaside "cottages," gentlemen's gambling clubs, bathhouses, and ice cream parlors. Cotillions, concerts, and other social gatherings filled the eight-week summer season.

At the turn of the 20th century, a band of Pittsburgh steel magnates came up with a new idea for the old seaside resort. The businessmen wanted to develop East Cape May into a "New Jersey Newport" - a resort catering to the wealthy and one that would rival Newport, Rhode Island. The centerpiece of their venture was a million dollar grand hotel. The project was doomed from the start.

Writer Jennifer Brownstone Kopp of the *Cape May Star and Wave* compares the history of the enormous hotel to that of the ill-fated *HMS Titanic*. Constructed during the same timeframe that brought forth the colossal ship, the brick hotel featured 333 rooms, central staircase, and glass domed ceiling, evocative of the design of the fateful *Titanic*.

The development was plagued with problems. Work stoppages because of racial conflicts delayed construction; building materials mysteriously disappeared. The dredge *Pittsburgh* sank while laboring to create the new harbor; her eight man crew just barely escaped. Tragedy struck when a workman fell from the roof plunging to his death.

The hotel opened two years late in 1908, but by then construction costs had doubled. The hotel was inexplicably shut down "for repairs" six months later. Project president Peter Shields withdrew from the enterprise and the remaining partners had no choice but to declare bankruptcy.

Others tried to make a go of the disastrous land project, (the next overseer met with death when a train hit his car), but ultimately the property was acquired by the U.S. Navy.

During both World Wars, the hotel was used as a hospital and housed hundreds of seriously wounded soldiers.

Another death occurred in the brick and steel edifice while the hotel operated as the Christian Admiral.

The story goes that a temperamental chef was chasing a waitress through the hotel. Perhaps it was only horseplay, but the young woman raced blindly to the lobby and entered an elevator. The chef could only watch in horror as the waitress unwittingly entered the car not knowing it had been removed for repairs. She fell to her death.

Before the building was razed in 1996, the aforementioned journalist, Jennifer Brownstone Kopp, photographically documented the interior. She snapped a time exposure in the lobby, the hub of activity in the once magnificent hotel. The photojournalist captured on the film what appears to be ectoplasm eerily revealing the profile of a woman. Many think this photo is tangible proof of the doomed waitress' spirit.

The Hotel Cape May was unceremoniously leveled on a cold, gray February day.

The contractor responsible for the clean up felt the site was a very strange place. Returning to the location each morning, it seemed to him as if the bricks and debris carted away the previous day had reappeared. He couldn't explain it.

Did the *building* that had once held so much promise and economic hope not want to leave? Was it the soul of the forsaken structure begging to stay… or was it the invisible ones inside?

*More than one spirit pervades the Peter Shields Inn.*

## PETER SHIELDS INN
1301 Beach Drive

Peter Shields was the first president of the ambitious East Cape May Project incorporated to turn the seaside town into an exclusive resort for the wealthy. In 1907 he built his stately home, today's Peter Shields Inn, to rival those erected in Newport, Rhode Island.

Although the development project never flourished, the Peter Shields Inn stands as a testament to its visionary designer. Furnished with exceptional antiques, the inn exudes an ambience of an earlier age.

Perhaps that is why Peter Shields' spirit stays behind haunting his former home. The staff differs on the identity of the gentle presence. Employees feel that the revenant who remains is the steel magnate's son.

At the turn of the 20th century, Cape May was noted for its strand of hard packed sand, the perfect platform for Henry Ford and Louis Chevrolet to showcase their automobiles. The two automakers, along with the members of the newly organized Cape May Automobile Club, participated in car races on the beach in front of the Hotel Cape May. These events were widely publicized and very popular contests.

Personal tragedy struck the Shields family when their son Earl was killed in a car accident during one of the competitions.

Having passed at a young age, his invisible wraith seems to be attracted mostly to the young girls who frequent the inn these days. His antics are subtle and teasing – he'll flip their hair or tap them on their shoulder.

Unexplainable phenomena in the basement includes lights going on and off without explanation. His palpable but unseen presence in the basement is so unnerving that female employees refuse to go down there alone.

The Hotel Cape May is no longer, the strand has eroded away, but what does remain is an outstanding edifice attesting to one man's dream. The nightmare of losing a son is long forgotten, but the young man's spirit lingers living the good life in his former abode, one of Cape May's outstanding B&Bs.

## THE WINDWARD HOUSE INN
24 Jackson Street

Jackson Street is the heart of Cape May's historic district and, according to a local ghost tour, is the *soul* of the resort town with no less than six haunted places on the block.

When Philadelphia lawyer George Baum put up a gracious Edwardian "shingle-style" house in 1907, Jackson Street was the main thoroughfare and led to the steamboat landing. Little did Baum know that his lovely home would someday harbor the ghost of a young woman.

Turned into a boarding house in the 1940s, the structure was transformed in 1977 into one of Cape May's original bed and breakfast inns.

The charming inn features three porches and a sundeck – a perfect blend for sun or shade.

Speaking of shades, the resident ghost is thought to be a former employee, a highly emotional Irish maid. An obscure Victorian poet described the Celtic character as playful, passionate, and sentimental. Is it any wonder that the third floor stays alive with her phantom frolics?

*The Windward House Inn is one of six haunted houses on Jackson Street.*

In the Wicker Room, and an adjoining space once used as servant's quarters, psychic investigator Dave Juliano of the South Jersey Ghost Research Organization captured eerie orbs on film. These balls of light are thought to be evidence of a ghostly energy and were prevalent in the hallway and staircase leading to the two rooms and near a wooden trunk.

One "scientific" theory for ghosts is that when extreme human emotions are experienced, electrical energy is discharged by the body and imbeds itself in the environs, like walls and furnishings. Gifted psychics can "read" the room or objects, a process called psychometry. Antiques, like the wooden trunk in this case, can be storehouses of information and provide a glimpse into the past.

The apparition of the Irish maid has been reported by a number of guests. When they describe their encounter, the malingering spirit is usually sitting on the edge of their bed.

Don't be put off by her presence though. She's an affable hostess and puts in appearances only to assure a pleasant stay.

*Esmerelda haunts the witch's hat turret room
at 22 Jackson Street.*

## THE INN AT 22 JACKSON

After the 1878 inferno that consumed a 30-acre expanse, the world's finest craftsmen were called on by the privileged to rebuild their summer homes. Cape May city's houses' sumptuous use of ornate gingerbread trim, stained glass windows, copious cupolas, towers and turrets are the result of neighbors trying to outdo each other.

For over fifty years a spirit named Esmerelda has outlived many a visitor at the eclectic inn at 22 Jackson Street. Her primary domain is the witch's hat turret room yet her welcoming spirit can be felt throughout the Victorian guesthouse.

Some have spied Esmerelda's specter sitting on their bed. Some have caught a glimpse of the ghost in their peripheral vision. Mostly, she manifests as a gentle presence who seems to particularly like children.

*A Native American's specter has been seen walking the paths of the popular Cold Spring Village.*

## SEA HOLLY INN
## 815 Stockton Street

This three-story "cottage" with distinctive Italianate detailing is furnished with authentic Renaissance Revival antiques. This type of architecture provides plenty of places for spirits to play hide'n seek inside this inn endowed with many cryptic goings-on.

According to psychics, one of the ghosts is a former female servant employed by the home's original owners. Several guests have witnessed her apparition - her specter lingers in one of the dormer rooms where a white haze hovers from time to time.

The only goal for 19th century girls was to marry and marry well. When photos were taken of a bride and groom on the inn's staircase, the image of an unidentified woman in Victorian dress stood behind them. This photo is on display at the Sea Holly Inn for anyone to see.

Psychics say the specter in the photograph was engaged to a well-to-do gentleman, was elated over their impending marriage, but died of a fever shortly before her wedding day.

*Who is the specter-in-waiting at the Sea Holly Inn?*

Others claim the servant girl's spirit stays behind waiting for her fiancé who was lost at sea.

When the previous owners were disturbed by the sound of footsteps on the upper floors when they started to renovate the property, they investigated the noise, but found no body up there.

Soon shadows started to appear in a window and in the hallway near the kitchen. Invisible hands moved the plants in the hall. Most of the abnormal activity occurred when no one else was in the house except for the proprietors.

Present co-owner Walt Melnick feels the talk of the ghostly goings on inside his house is a "bunch of hooey" and insists his house is *not* haunted. Instead, he considers the Sea Holly Inn an "enchanted cottage" and welcomes anyone to photograph the ghostly picture and listen to the eerie audiotape of electronic voice phenomena recorded at the dwelling.

Melnick calls himself a non-believer and has not had any experiences outside the norm.

Psychic Jane Dougherty writes extensively of her experiences at the Sea Holly Inn. Visit her website www.janedougherty.com – a must read!

*Spectral energy exudes from the Thorn and the Rose.*

## THORN & THE ROSE
822 Stockton Street

When a psychic arrived at the Thorn & The Rose, she was struck by the eerie energy generated by the 1868 guest suites. The twin Italianate style inn with carefully tended gardens didn't *look* haunted. But a strong ethereal impression captured the medium's interest.

The owners were well aware of what was going on inside; as soon as they moved in, mysterious shadows appeared in all the wrong places. Room 2 harbored an unidentifiable female phantom who appeared exclusively to the male guests.

Most uncanny was that when Cape May's fire siren signaled, sounds of a bouncing ball began in an upstairs hallway. At odd times it sounded like a child's wagon was being pulled along the floor.

The psychic medium "read" the building and discerned *a little boy who was terrified of fire was bouncing a ball to relieve his anxiety.* The psychic also saw the boy pulling a toy wagon!

Sea salt, since sprinkled around the structure's foundation, has stilled the spectral activity.

*Certain members of the Physick Family refuse to leave their magnificent estate. Who can blame them!*

## EMLEN PHYSICK ESTATE
1048 Washington Street

The Mid-Atlantic Center (MAC) for the Arts, founded in 1970 expressly to rescue the 18-room Emlen Physick Estate from demolition, operates New Jersey's only Victorian house museum.

When the Stick Style house was completed in 1879, Emlen Physick Jr., his mother, Frances Ralston, and his aunt, Emilie Parmentier moved into their home. Emlen, who never married, was the grandson of Dr. Philip Syng Physick, a wealthy and famous Philadelphian, who is considered the "father of American surgery."

Emlen was a graduate of medical school but never practiced medicine. He owned two farms and lived the life of a gentleman farmer, grazing livestock at his Washington Street estate.

Although MAC will not admit it, rumor has it that the spirits of both Emlen and his mom are active in the house. Their manifestations are subtle except for the time Mrs. Ralston's wheelchair chased a staff member out of her room according to *Cape May Ghost Stories, Book Two.*

*Fine dining and "spirits" at the Washington Inn.*

## WASHINGTON INN
Washington & Jefferson Streets

The Washington Inn is nestled on tree-lined Washington Street in the heart of the historic district. Built in 1840 as a Plantation home, the inn has been owned by the Craig family for three generations. The inn offers five· unique dining rooms from patio dining to cozy fireside tables.

Already one hundred years old when opened as an inn in the 1940s, the building was renovated many times. Part of its history includes a move to another position on the property, only to be returned to its original setting.

Like every Cape May wraith, the Washington Inn is home to a friendly ghost. The foyer was once the most haunted spot where the resident unseen spirit, christened "Elizabeth," would often call out to employees by name. Since the central staircase was removed, she has quieted down, although some still claim to hear her soft whisperings. Elizabeth may be mute, but the shattering of drinking glasses remains a mystery at the historic haunted inn.

*An ethereal Esther still parties at the Southern Mansion.*

## SOUTHERN MANSION
720 Washington Street

*The Southern Mansion* lithograph that hangs in wealthy Philadelphia industrialist George Allen's former home was the inspiration for the gracious hospitality offered at this grand seaside palace.

It's hard to imagine than more than fifty years ago, the splendid estate operated as a boarding house. The property was poorly maintained and shut down in the 1980s.

The building languished until 1994 when the present owners were vacationing in Cape May. Shocked and saddened at the sight of the deteriorating structure on the sprawling grounds, they made a commitment to bring the Italianate masterpiece back to life. The renovation seemed to have enlivened George Allen's niece, Esther, as well.

Guests have reported seeing her reflection in mirrors. They have heard her laughter and the rustle of her skirts as she dances to ghostly music. Most of all, the hallmark of her unmistakable presence is the scent of her expensive perfume. The invisible lady continues to enjoy her long ago pleasures.

*Winterwood Gift Shoppe on the Washington Street Mall has a spectral stock boy named "Charlie."*

## WINTERWOOD GIFT SHOPPES

The building that houses the Winterwood Gift Shoppe on the Washington Street Mall originally quartered Dr. Loomis' dental office and the Knerr sisters' millinery shop.

When the shop operated as Keltie's News and Books the owners witnessed a white-coated apparition wandering the building. At times, books literally flew off the shelves then disembodied giggling followed – the sound of tittering girls pulling a childish prank. Some attribute the high jinx to the Knerr sisters.

The present resident ghost is nicknamed "Charlie." After eager shoppers have called it a day and stock girls refill the shelves Charlie gives them a hard time by hiding merchandise. His presence is palpable in the stock room and his footsteps can be heard even during the busiest times of the day.

Strangely enough, another pair of spectral sisters haunts the original WINTERWOOD GIFT SHOPPE on Route 9 in Rio Grande. In fact, the store is *so* haunted that a sign warns all who enter of the unseen specters lurking within.

The haunting story at the Rio Grande store revolves around the Hildreth family, one of the founding families of Cape May. Joshua Hildreth built the house in 1722 and the last descendants to reside there were two spinster sisters, Hester and Lucille, who died in 1948 and 1954 respectively. Inseparable when alive, they remain together in the afterlife at their ancestral home. Their soft voices and footsteps infiltrate the house and their shadowy forms have been discerned inside and out.

Reports of a white-robed phantom gliding across the lawn to the family burial ground out back are legendary. As the wraith reaches the graveyard, she simply fades away.

The Hildreth's housed a colonial soldier. To show his gratitude, he fashioned a beautifully carved mantelpiece that remains intact inside the gift shop. Sensitives feel his spirit remains inside the shop as well still proud of his handiwork.

Otherworldly occurrences include merchandise disappearing and reappearing, unexplainable noises and most mystifying, employees watch in wonder as store displays dismantle before their eyes.

Visit this lovely boutique and perhaps you'll have a brush with the souls that once inhabited this historic place.

*The original Winterwood Gift Shoppe in Rio Grande remains the otherworldly home of the Hildreth sisters.*

*The Doctors Inn held the remedy for those travelling the Underground Railroad.*

## THE DOCTORS INN
2 North Main Street
Cape May Court House

Located in the center of Cape May Court House, Cape May's county seat, is the beautifully restored, 19th century, Doctors Inn.

The property's recorded history dates back to a 1690 land grant to colonial physician, Dr. Cox.

Dr. John Wiley and his wife Danielia built the stately home in 1854 and saw their house as a refuge to those making their way north along the Underground Railroad. Tunnels used by escaped slaves on their way to freedom are still evident in the basement.

Having housed and helped so many, by the 1980s the building was in need of salvation itself.

Doctor Carolyn Crawford, a neonatologist, revived the failing property and along with a team of dedicated and talented professionals brought the dwelling back to life.

The restoration resuscitated some former inhabitants as well. Some have spotted the apparition of a lively little girl running through the rooms. Her dress is from an earlier era and a large bow is prominent in her long blond hair. She likes to open and close doors.

Throughout the three-story house, cabinets and drawers are often found open.

It seems that the inn's dining areas are hot spots for paranormal activity. South Jersey Ghost Research representatives, using an infrared camera, captured ectoplasm swirling in the corners of the rooms. Both inside and out, orbs of light manifest in photos, attesting to a ghostly presence.

Visitors have observed a male apparition and discerned unexplainable sounds on the second floor. Could this be John Wiley, M.D. continuing his routine in the afterlife? His portrait hangs in his former examining room where his spirit is palpable and also sometimes manifests.

Others have witnessed the apparition of a lady in red outside walking about the inn's property.

*The pre-Revolutionary War John Holmes House at 504 Route 9, Cape May Court House, is home to the spirit of its namesake builder. Employees and visitors at the county museum have encountered the apparition of a man and heard his deep voice.*

*The Queen's Hotel – haunted by the restless spirits of Cape May's colorful past.*

## QUEEN'S HOTEL
### 601 Columbia Avenue

At the corner of Columbia and Ocean Avenues is the recently restored Queen's Hotel. The building has a colorful history, which includes an incarnation as a drugstore, a fancy gambling hall, and a brothel.

Brothels were essential elements of the Victorian life; 8,000 flourished in London while only 4 churches existed!

Although presently the haunting activity seems to have quieted down, in the past an unknown entity, thought to be a "lady of the evening," sought attention in a variety of ways.

When the hotel operated as the Heirloom Inn, the third floor was the center of paranormal activity. In the Plum and Palm Rooms an unseen presence, exuding a strong scent of heavy perfume, would sometimes bump up against the beds.

Objects and furniture changed position in the rooms when no *(mortal)* body had been in the chambers. Not surprisingly, when the building was a brothel, the call girls' lodgings were on the third floor!

*The specter of a Confederate soldier bunks at the Brass Bed.*

## THE BRASS BED
719 Columbia Avenue

This Gothic Revival style structure was known as the Lewis Tannenbaum House and was constructed circa 1872 with a distinctive third story central gable ornamented with a large hanging pendant.

During the Civil War, some Cape May houses were temporary quarters for both Confederate *and* Union armed forces. For the most part, Cape May hostelries pledged no allegiance to either side, mostly for the sake of economic endurance.

Surviving inside the Brass Bed Inn is the spirit of a long dead Confederate soldier. Those who have encountered his revenant are chilled to the bone when the full-bodied apparition asks, *"Who won the war!"*

The engaging spectral soldier seems to know the conflict is over and we can only surmise that he lingers at his Columbia Avenue lodgings because he enjoys his visitations, although infrequent, to his favorite post mortem vacation destination.

*The John F. Craig House has an accommodating spirit.*

## JOHN F. CRAIG HOUSE
609 Columbia Avenue

The 1866 Carpenter Gothic John F. Craig House is nestled in the heart of the historic district. John Fullerton Craig, a Philadelphia sugar broker, purchased the gingerbread house in 1891 as a summer home.

The bed and breakfast inn boasts spacious rooms and the French doors, surrounding the parlor and dining room, provide cool and refreshing sea breezes. Period antiques, original gasoliers light fixtures and reproduction period wallpapers adorn the airy interior and create an authentic "Gay Nineties" ambiance.

A good-natured presence permeates this guesthouse and the unseen spirit feels right at home in this atmosphere of earlier days.

The center of spectral activity is Room #5, once the servant's room and named after Lucy Johnson, the Craig's longtime cook.

One guest had readied a needle and thread to sew a button on her slacks but hadn't gotten around to it. When she returned to her room, the mending had been done. She thanked one of the owners, Connie Felicetti for the kindness, but Connie was miffed – she hadn't fixed the button, nor had anyone on the staff. No body else had the key to the room…

Another guest claimed that she was prompted to take her medication by an invisible hand when a dish of potpourri fell off the bed stand in the middle of the night and woke her up. The incident was the trigger she needed to remember the medicine.

These thoughtful acts are attributed to Lucy Johnson's accommodating and faithful spirit.

Another phantom fond of the Victorian home is a red-haired little girl. When the youngster appeared in Room #4, the Susan Craig Room, she was seen standing at the foot of the bed.

## "LIGHT OF ASIA"

In 1884, a strange sight began to appear on the meadows between the city of Cape May and Cape May Point. Day by day the wooden creature grew into a pachyderm called the "Light of Asia."

Hundreds of people arrived by excursion trains and boats to Cape May to see this 40 foot high colossal oddity. Entering the hind legs, a spiral staircase led to a small concession stand inside and access to the howdah observatory that provided a scenic ocean view. Refreshments were also served from the front legs of the structure.

Despite her popularity, the concept was a financial disaster - receipts never covered the $18,000 cost of construction.

The "Light of Asia" was left empty and abandoned by 1887. But was the deteriorating landmark really vacant?

Before her remains were condemned and cremated on May 26, 1900, the "Light of Asia" was the subject of a newspaper report that stated, "strange sounds emanated" from the relic and hinted that the hulking beast was haunted.

*Author's note: "Lucy," the Margate Elephant is the closest and only surviving relative to South Cape May's "Light of Asia".*

*Listen carefully for ghostly voices at this waterfront eatery.*

## CABANAS
### Beach and Decatur Streets

This waterfront restaurant operates out of a four-story Victorian building constructed in 1879. The last stop on the Original Haunted Cape May Ghost Tour, the story behind the haunting presence is that a woman committed suicide by hanging herself on the third floor landing.

Al Rauber, originator of the ghost tour, has investigated the mysterious third-floor happenings, which have plagued the place for decades. During the probe he captured on audiotape the eerie otherworldly voice of a woman saying, "She's pretty." Rauber's partner, Diane Bixler, was the only female present in the room at the time.

The building has hosted a large number of businesses and each new renovation brings the spirit of the long dead woman back to life. She can be heard, but not seen, moving about the rooms.

There are those who claim the mysterious spirit can also be felt in the distinctive cupola atop the building.

*The Hotel Macomber wait staff includes a female phantom.*

## HOTEL MACOMBER
### 727 Beach Avenue

The Hotel Macomber was the last historic landmark building to be constructed in Cape May. At the time, the grand shingle-style mansion was the largest frame structure east of the Mississippi.

Today it is home to the Union Park restaurant and, some say, two female phantoms.

Room 10 is famous for paranormal incidents. During the night guests awake to the sound of dresser drawers opening and closing. Lights turn on and off by themselves and the bathroom doorknob turns when no one else is in the room.

The mysterious activity is attributed to a former hotel guest who loved the old hotel and was a frequent visitor. It seems as if her spirit is going about her routine unaware of present day guests.

The other phantom is probably a 1930s era waitress who choked to death on a chicken bone after she swiped the fowl off a diner's dinner plate. Her spirit was in a foul mood the day she pushed a kitchen worker against the shelves in the walk-in refrigerator.

## HIGBEE BEACH
Cape May Point

The tangled terrain and eerie cries of unseen animals and birds hiding themselves in the marshy pools echo in the ethers along this desolate stretch of bayshore beach. A popular spot for fishermen, birdwatchers, sunbathers, and *ghosts*, the isolated shoreline is a perfect setting for a haunting...

A long held legend is that phantom pirates still guard their treasure buried on the coast long ago.

Another oft-told tale is that the beach is the otherworldly stomping ground for plantation owner Old Man Higbee. The story goes that Higbee was buried face down so that he could meet Satan face to face. Sometimes at dawn's first light, his luminous apparition glides over the dunes and into the surf.

Another soul stuck between dimensions is Higbee's personal slave. Charged in life to keep watch over his master's grave, he continues his vigil to this very day.

*Sunrise specters stroll about the Cape May Point Light.*

## CAPE MAY POINT LIGHT

Fishermen and early morning walkers have encountered mysterious ramblers along the beach and at the Cape May Point Light.

Visitors to the light think they see kindred spirits taking a sunrise stroll. In fact they do, but the spirits are non-responsive, detached, and in another dimension, an "other" world of their own.

The present lighthouse beacon, first lit on Halloween in 1859, is fully operational and has been automated since 1946.

For over one hundred years, visitors to Cape May have made it a tradition to venture to the Point, just two miles away, and make the climb up the 199 spiraling stairs to catch a dizzying view of the seaside from a seagull's perspective.

Since 1986, the Mid-Atlantic Center for the Arts (MAC) has been responsible for the light and operating the historic site as a museum. Most at MAC deny the existence of members of the nether world perambulating about the light, but those who have witnessed the ghostly goings on swear that spirits swarm about the antique light.

## WORLD WAR II BUNKER
Cape May Point

During World War II, enemy submarines lurked off the New Jersey coast. To protect the coastline, the US Army Corps of Engineers constructed the cement gun emplacement bunker that stands just east of the Cape May Point Light.

Equipped like any other fort, men were stationed inside the underground battery to ward off any foreign U-boats entering our waters.

The cement hulk was camouflaged, hidden under sand and, at that time, stood on dry land. Time and tides have exposed the hideaway and revealed the spectral sailors still living inside their concrete haunt peering out the gun ports.

When the public had access to the bunker, some claim uncanny encounters. They witnessed spectral sailors performing their duty inside and outside the edifice. Eerie conversations were heard, but could not be deciphered. Lighters flared as ethereal cigarettes were lit.

These men, so devoted to duty, remain on guard long after they have passed away.

*The World War II bunker will forever remain a part of Cape May's haunted history.*

## CLOSING THOUGHTS...

The realm of spirits is mystifying and to offer a rational explanation for the intangible is a daunting task. The ghostly census for Cape May County hovers near *one hundred* (!) according to parapsychologist Al Rauber. Rauber claims there is a connection between electromagnetic fields (EMF) and ghosts. Utilizing high-tech equipment, he finds Cape May's EMF is *unusually* high.

Tourists will continue to tell inexplicable tales of uncanny experiences in their summer rentals, like the one about the ghostly Victorian family who left little piles of buttons all over the house.

Cape May's ghostly yarns have been passed along for decades and the stories, like the spirits themselves, will live on for eons.

Young, old, rich, poor, famous and nameless - Cape May's resident revenants makes this a city of mystery where it's hard to tell the difference between past and present. Any season is shadow time in this seaside town where it's easy to understand why so many long dead live on in this enchanting location.

# BIBLIOGRAPHY

*ARTICLES:*
Kopp, Jennifer Brownstone, "Spirited Cape May – More than Meets the Eye." *Cape May Star and Wave*, Cape May, NJ; October 2000.

_____. "Ghosts in Cape May.  Do You Believe?" *Cape May Star and Wave*, Cape May, NJ; October 2000.

_____, "Searching for Henry Sawyer, the Past Comes Alive." *Cape May Star and Wave, Cape May, NJ*; 1999.

_____, "Cape May's Own Titanic, Watching History Go Away." *Cape May Star and Wave*, Cape May, NJ; February 26, 1996.

Urgo, Jacqueline L., "Tapping into the Spirit of Cape May." *Philadelphia Inquirer*, Philadelphia, PA; February 29, 1996.

*BOOKS:*
Adams, Charles J. III, *Cape May Ghost Stories, Book Two.* Exeter House Books, Reading, PA; 1997.

Cudworth, Marsha, *Self-Guided Architectural Tours, Cape May N.J.* Lady Raspberry Press, New York, NY; 1997.

Hauck, Dennis William, *Haunted Places: The National Directory.* Penguin Books USA Inc., New York, NY; 1996.

Salvini, Emil R., *The Summer City by the Sea*. Wheal-Grace Publications, Belleville, NJ; 1995.

Seibold, David J. & Adams, Charles J. III, *Cape May Ghost Stories*. Exeter House Books, Barnegat Light, NJ & Reading, PA; 1988.

WEBSITES:
Angel of the Sea: www.AngeloftheSea.com
Cape May: www.capemay.com
Cape May and Ghosts: www.jerseyshore.org
Colvmns by the Sea: www.Colvmns.com
The Doctors Inn Bed & Breakfast: www.doctorsinn.com
Emlen Physick Estate: capemaymac.org/Physick-Estate
Haunted New Jersey: www.hauntednewjersey.com
Jane Dougherty: www.janedougherty.com
The John F. Craig House: www.johnfcraig.com
Lucy the Elephant: www.lucytheelephant.org
The Peter Shields Inn: www.petershieldsinn.com
Queen's Hotel: www.QueensHotel.com
Sea Holly Inn Bed & Breakfast: www.SeaHollyInn.com
The Southern Mansion: www.SouthernMansion.net
Thorn and the Rose: www.thornandtherose.com
Windward House Inn: www.windwardhouseinn.com

# CAPE MAY

# GHOST WALKS

Original Haunted Cape May Tours

609-463-8984

Haunted Mansion Ghost Tours

609-884-1199

# HAUNTED CAPE MAY

Other books by

## *Lynda Lee Macken*

GHOSTS OF THE GARDEN STATE
GHOSTLY GOTHAM
HAUNTED SALEM & BEYOND
ADIRONDACK GHOSTS
HAUNTED HISTORY OF STATEN ISLAND

For purchasing information contact:

BLACK CAT PRESS
Post Office Box 1218
Forked River, New Jersey 08731

*Email*
llmacken@hotmail.com

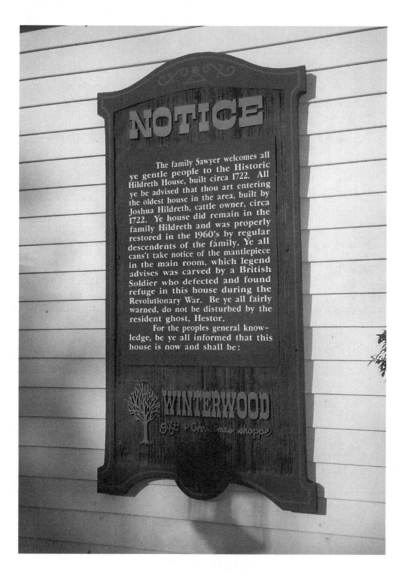

*Some places in Cape May are so haunted that signs warn of unseen specters lurking within…*